AS A MAN THINKETH

A
personal notebook
with quotes from
the inspirational classic
by James Allen

RUNNING PRESS
PHILADELPHIA, PENNSYLVANIA

Canadian representatives: General Publishing Co., Ltd., 30 Lesmill Road, Don Mills, Ontario M3B 2T6.

International representatives: Worldwide Media Services, Inc., 115 East Twenty-third Street, New York, New York 10010.

ISBN 1-56138-093-8

Cover design by Toby Schmidt
Interior design by Stephanie Longo
Interior illustrations by Brian Willette
Typography: CG Bodoni by Commcor Communications Corporation, Philadelphia, Pennsylvania
Printed in The United States of America

This book may be ordered by mail from the publisher. Please add $2.50 for postage and handling. *But try your bookstore first!*

Running Press Book Publishers
125 South Twenty-second Street
Philadelphia, Pennsylvania 19103

As a being of power, intelligence, and love, and the lord of his own thoughts, man holds the key to every situation, and contains within himself that transforming and regenerative agency by which he may make himself what he wills.

ONLY BY MUCH SEARCHING AND MINING ARE GOLD
AND DIAMONDS OBTAINED, AND MAN CAN FIND EVERY TRUTH
CONNECTED WITH HIS BEING IF HE WILL DIG DEEP INTO THE
MINE OF HIS SOUL. . . .

H E THAT SEEKETH FINDETH; AND TO HIM THAT
KNOCKETH IT SHALL BE OPENED. . ."

A MAN'S MIND MAY BE LIKENED TO A GARDEN,
WHICH MAY BE INTELLIGENTLY CULTIVATED OR ALLOWED TO
RUN WILD...

. . . A MAN SOONER OR LATER DISCOVERS THAT HE IS THE
MASTER GARDENER OF HIS SOUL, THE DIRECTOR OF HIS LIFE.

THOUGHT AND CHARACTER ARE ONE, AND AS
CHARACTER CAN ONLY MANIFEST AND DISCOVER ITSELF
THROUGH ENVIRONMENT AND CIRCUMSTANCE, THE OUTER
CONDITIONS OF A PERSON'S LIFE WILL ALWAYS BE FOUND TO
BE HARMONIOUSLY RELATED TO HIS INNER STATE.

EVERY MAN IS WHERE HE IS BY THE LAW OF
HIS BEING. . .

Every thought seed sown or allowed to fall into the mind, and to take root there, produces its own, blossoming sooner or later into act, and bearing its own fruitage of opportunity and circumstance.

As the reaper of his own harvest, man learns both by suffering and bliss.

CIRCUMSTANCE DOES NOT MAKE THE MAN; IT
REVEALS HIM TO HIMSELF.

MEN DO NOT ATTRACT THAT WHICH THEY *WANT*, BUT
THAT WHICH THEY *ARE*.

NOT WHAT HE WISHES AND PRAYS FOR DOES A MAN GET, BUT WHAT HE JUSTLY EARNS.

MEN ARE ANXIOUS TO IMPROVE THEIR CIRCUM-
STANCES, BUT ARE UNWILLING TO IMPROVE THEMSELVES;
THEY THEREFORE REMAIN BOUND.

. . .THE CONDITIONS OF HAPPINESS VARY SO VASTLY
WITH INDIVIDUALS, THAT A MAN'S *ENTIRE* SOUL CONDITION
(ALTHOUGH IT MAY BE KNOWN TO HIMSELF) CANNOT BE JUDGED
BY ANOTHER FROM THE EXTERNAL ASPECT OF HIS LIFE ALONE.

Good thoughts and actions can never produce bad results; bad thoughts and actions can never produce good results.

BLESSEDNESS AND RICHES ARE ONLY JOINED
TOGETHER WHEN THE RICHES ARE RIGHTLY AND WISELY
USED. . .

A MAN CANNOT *DIRECTLY* CHOOSE HIS CIRCUMSTANCES, BUT HE CAN CHOOSE HIS THOUGHTS, AND SO INDIRECTLY, YET SURELY, SHAPE HIS CIRCUMSTANCES.

THE WORLD IS YOUR KALEIDOSCOPE, AND THE VARYING COMBINATIONS OF COLORS WHICH AT EVERY SUCCEEDING MOMENT IT PRESENTS TO YOU ARE THE EXQUISITELY ADJUSTED PICTURES OF YOUR EVER-MOVING THOUGHTS.

THE BODY IS THE SERVANT OF THE MIND.

THE BODY IS A DELICATE AND PLASTIC INSTRUMENT, WHICH RESPONDS READILY TO THE THOUGHTS BY WHICH IT IS IMPRESSED, AND HABITS OF THOUGHT WILL PRODUCE THEIR OWN EFFECTS, GOOD OR BAD, UPON IT.

THERE IS NO PHYSICIAN LIKE CHEERFUL THOUGHT FOR DISSIPATING THE ILLS OF THE BODY; THERE IS NO COMFORTER TO COMPARE WITH GOOD WILL FOR DISPERSING THE SHADOWS OF GRIEF AND SORROW.

Until thought is linked with purpose there is no intelligent accomplishment.

THEY WHO HAVE NO CENTRAL PURPOSE IN THEIR LIFE FALL AN EASY PREY TO PETTY WORRIES, FEARS, TROUBLES, AND SELF-PITYINGS. . .

A MAN SHOULD CONCEIVE OF A LEGITIMATE
PURPOSE IN HIS HEART, AND SET OUT TO ACCOMPLISH IT.

HE WILL TO DO STEMS FROM THE KNOWLEDGE THAT WE *CAN* DO.

HE WHO HAS CONQUERED DOUBT AND FEAR HAS CONQUERED FAILURE.

He who has conquered weakness, and has put away all selfish thoughts, belongs neither to oppressor nor oppressed. He is free.

THERE CAN BE NO PROGRESS, NO ACHIEVEMENT, WITHOUT SACRIFICE . . .

INTELLECTUAL ACHIEVEMENTS ARE THE RESULT OF
THOUGHT CONSECRATED TO THE SEARCH FOR KNOWLEDGE, OR
FOR THE BEAUTIFUL AND TRUE IN LIFE AND NATURE.

A CHIEVEMENT, OF WHATEVER KIND, IS THE CROWN
OF EFFORT, THE DIADEM OF THOUGHT.

Aᴸᴸ ACHIEVEMENTS, WHETHER IN THE BUSINESS,
INTELLECTUAL, OR SPIRITUAL WORLD, ARE THE RESULTS OF
DEFINITELY DIRECTED THOUGHT.

He who would accomplish little must sacrifice little; he who would achieve much must sacrifice much; he who would attain highly must sacrifice greatly.

THE DREAMERS ARE THE SAVIORS OF THE WORLD.

COMPOSER, SCULPTOR, PAINTER, POET, PROPHET, SAGE, THESE ARE THE MAKERS OF THE AFTERWORLD, THE ARCHITECTS OF HEAVEN.

E WHO CHERISHES A BEAUTIFUL VISION, A LOFTY
IDEAL IN HIS HEART, WILL ONE DAY REALIZE IT.

CHERISH YOUR VISIONS; CHERISH YOUR IDEALS. . .

 T O DESIRE IS TO OBTAIN; TO ASPIRE IS TO ACHIEVE.

THE GREATEST ACHIEVEMENT WAS AT FIRST AND FOR A TIME A DREAM.

Your circumstances may be uncongenial, but they shall not long remain so if you but perceive an ideal and strive to reach it.

"Gifts," powers, material, intellectual, and spiritual possessions are the fruits of effort; they are thoughts completed, objects accomplished, visions realized.

THE VISION THAT YOU GLORIFY IN YOUR MIND, THE IDEAL THAT YOU ENTHRONE IN YOUR HEART—THIS YOU WILL BUILD YOUR LIFE BY, THIS YOU WILL BECOME.

 ALMNESS OF MIND IS ONE OF THE BEAUTIFUL JEWELS OF WISDOM.

THAT EXQUISITE POISE OF CHARACTER WHICH WE
CALL SERENITY IS THE LAST LESSON OF CULTURE; IT IS THE
FLOWERING OF LIFE, THE FRUITAGE OF THE SOUL.